THE HIST
KING LEAR
AND HIS THREE
DAUGHTERS

WILLIAM
SHAKESPEARE

Abridged by John Short

THE PURPOSE OF SHOTS

If our written culture is to prosper, it cannot just feed off an intellectual readership: it must attract a wider audience enthusiastically into its fold. It is exactly this which we wish to help achieve with *Shots*.

Shots are summaries of books you want, or need, to read, without having to plough through hundreds of pages. They are designed to deliver maximum effect with minimum effort – but not, please note, no effort at all. As Albert Einstein said, everything should be made as simple as possible, but not simpler.

If your spare time is limited, by taking in a few *Shots* you can greatly expand your repertoire and knowledge of books that interest you. Some may be technically demanding or require specialist knowledge to appreciate or understand them in the original (e.g. Darwin's *Origin of Species*). Again, a *Shot* is the answer – and may yet inspire you to go on to read the full version.

Each *Shot* is an intelligent, concentrated synthesis of a significant piece of writing. Nearly all the hard work has been done for you: reduced to around 25 pages of summary, and covering a wide range of subjects of general and specialist interest – from literature to philosophy, from arts to sciences, and from the past to the present – it will take just an hour or so to read.

For the growing list of available titles, to suggest others, or to pass comment, please visit our website at **www.shots.co.uk**.

SHOTS
Straight to the point

22 Mount Ephraim Road,
Tunbridge Wells, TN1 1ED

Shots is a registered trade mark of Velocity Blue Limited in the UK and in certain other countries

Published in the UK by Velocity Blue Limited

© John R W Short 2014

Design by **CantateCommunications.com**
Identity and design: Jon Ashby.
King Lear illustration: David Jordan.

ISBN **978-1-910897-03-4**

Version 1.3

CONTENTS

INTRODUCTION
TO SHAKESPEARE SHOTS

Like all the *Shots* we publish, *Shakespeare Shots* are intended to give you the essence, and not a dilution, of the underlying work. They do not aim to compete with it on literary merit. With writing as masterful as Shakespeare's, it is pretty well impossible to echo the artistry of the original. But, *Shots* do provide clear, bite-sized renderings of great literature, combined with a feel for the underlying work (helped by quotations matched directly to the summary) which are informative and interesting in their own right, and which may tempt you further.

The purist and the specialist might ask, "Why not just read the original?" But they would be missing the point. Sometimes we need help. Or, our priorities might lie elsewhere, though we still wish to expand our knowledge into other areas. Or again, a considerate introduction will ultimately bring more fruitful results than being whacked over the head with a 300 page text right at the start. An endless significance lies in reading, but many have been terminally put off by exactly this kind of approach.

We hope that *Shakespeare Shots* will help make these great plays accessible to a wider audience of enquiring minds, and encourage greater familiarity with them either by going on to read Shakespeare in the original or, as intended by the playwright, seeing his plays on stage.

The quotations referenced in the summary of each scene and presented on the facing page may well sound familiar, including as they do several phrases still in common usage. Look out for them – this is where they came from – a small reflection of Shakespeare's genius. He is a playwright who speaks our language as well as his own, and this realisation may encourage those who are daunted by them to allow his plays to work their magic and enjoy them for what they are.

It can't be helped: the summaries are, of course, subjective. This is part of the fun, and brings them to life more than would otherwise be the case. It will also encourage the reader to generate his or her own thoughts about the play – and who knows what that will lead on to?

CONTINUED...

No, there are no explanatory notes or annotations. Rather, there is space for you to write down your own thoughts and comments. *Shots* can prompt your own ideas, be a quick and useful way of reading around the subject (other titles by the same author), or even a speedy revision guide. Whichever way, make it your own; it's cheap, portable, and can be appreciated in its own right.

The plot is here for you, some of the magnificent language and more famous quotations are here for you, and together they serve as an introduction to one of the greatest pieces of literature in the English language. For many of you, this *Shot* will provide ninety per cent of what you require for, dare we say it, ten per cent of the effort – and in a memorable format. For some, it will provoke an interest and a desire to read more.

For others, it will open up a whole new world.

KING LEAR

INTRODUCTION
TO KING LEAR

Watching *King Lear* on stage is like being put through a mangle; after much pain, all the hopes we might have that a Guiding Hand will ensure that life's trials and sufferings will eventually be balanced by redeeming benefits are relentlessly squeezed out of us. If anything, it is the Hand itself that is turning the mangle or, as Kent puts it, "the rack of this tough world".

Lacking civilised or philosophical restraints, those characters with the power to do so behave brutally and excessively. Human considerations do not act as a break: an old man's eyes are plucked out, brother plots the death of brother, sister poisons sister, dog eats dog. Most characters respond with ferocity, and without understanding, mercy, or forgiveness. Man is cruel and superstitious, but at the same time feeble.

This is the nature of the particular world which Shakespeare forces us to observe in *King Lear*. Whether or not that's what the "real" world is like, if such a thing exists, is one of the debates which emerges from the play. It seems, though, that Shakespeare believes we are deluding ourselves if we think that life is any different to his representation of it here. That's just the way things are. His scepticism runs deep, and is uncomfortable. It has nothing to do with right and wrong – justice itself is impossible to administer – and absolutely for certain it has nothing to do with right triumphing over wrong, or good over evil. The process is much more random than that.

And how far from being no more than beasts, unguided by moral precepts, has mankind progressed? The play is certainly not a celebration of god-like human intellect. There is, in fact, a sharp divide between helpless man and the gods. But, the divide between us and the brutal natural world is not as great as we might like to think. Our protection from it is fragile, and our cruelties, including cruelties of the mind, are harsher; Goneril and Regan lack "human" sympathy. If we reject civilisation, we quickly become bestial.

King Lear was written sometime between 1603 and 1606, just ten years or so before Shakespeare's death. It is clear from the play that he had by this time grown sadder and lest optimistic – as, perhaps, we all do – and his own catastrophes, whatever they were, must have contributed to this pessimism. Yet it is not all negative, and Lear himself is not without heroism: confronting and defying the inexplicable, ungovernable forces of nature, outstaring the emptiness, with a strange mixture of relish and tragic indignation; but never resignation.

This is a battle, a universal struggle which he can almost survive. What gets him, though, tearing his heart and his mind at the same time, is his treatment at the hands of his daughters Goneril and Regan, and of course his guilt over Cordelia and her subsequent death. On top of the emptiness, cruelty, injustice, human insignificance, and all the other generalised hopelessness, comes his personal tragedy – and it is the pain of that which drives him mad.

Although we can empathise with that trait of human nature, it's not exactly easy to sit back and enjoy *King Lear*, at least not in the obvious sense of enjoyment. We can appreciate it, sure; it is a very great play, but it is by no means a fairy tale. And the question it asks is a tough one: if we are brave enough to observe human dealings in a universe stripped of our protective illusions ("the excellent foppery of the world", as Edmund expresses it), does that make us better off than deriving false comfort from make-believe?

Do we want Shakespeare's *Lear*, or Nahum Tate's*? The choice is ours.

In 1681 Nahum Tate reworked the play to give it a happy ending: King Lear was returned to the throne and Cordelia, instead of dying, married Edgar.

LIST OF ROLES

LEAR *King of Britain*

GONERIL *His eldest daughter*

REGAN *His second daughter*

CORDELIA *His youngest daughter*

DUKE OF ALBANY *Married to Goneril*

DUKE OF CORNWALL *Married to Regan*

KING OF FRANCE

DUKE OF BURGUNDY

EARL OF GLOUCESTER

EDGAR *His elder son*

EDMUND *His younger bastard son*

EARL OF KENT

FOOL *Attendant on Lear*

OSWALD *Goneril's steward*

CURAN *A follower of Gloucester*

OLD MAN *Gloucester's tenant*

A Herald, a Captain, an Officer, Knights, Gentlemen, Attendants, Servants and Messengers

OVERALL PLOT SUMMARY

The complex action of *King Lear* takes place in pre-Roman, pre-Christian Britain, devoid, one supposes, of the civilising effects of either influence. We the audience are parachuted into an already developing chain of events, as if we have landed onto a moving conveyor belt, and we had better keep up.

The aged and irascible King Lear has summoned his court, including the loyal Earls of Kent and Gloucester, to witness the division of his kingdom between his three daughters, Goneril, Regan and Cordelia (in descending order of age). The first two are married to the Dukes of Albany and Cornwall respectively, but the youngest, and her father's favourite, is today to be promised to one of two suitors: the King of France or the Duke of Burgundy.

Lear wishes at the same time to abrogate all monarchical responsibility whilst retaining his status and privileges; equally absurdly, he requires as part of the formal procedure each of his daughters to stand up and announce in turn how much she loves him.

Goneril and Regan flatter their father with exaggerated protestations of love, but Cordelia (perhaps unwisely) refuses to play the game, and her measured but sincere response provokes him to an angry and unwarranted rejection of her; he divides her dowry between his other two daughters. France, unlike Burgundy, willingly accepts Cordelia dowerless, and she leaves with him. Kent is banished for bravely defending her in front of a court stunned by the king's misjudgement. Goneril and Regan, only too aware of Lear's foibles, dislike his plans to divide his time between them, as well as his expensive requirement of a retinue of 100 knights.

Edmund, handsome illegitimate son of Gloucester, is resentful that his legitimate elder brother Edgar will inherit their father's estate, and plans his own advancement by convincing the superstitious Gloucester that Edgar is plotting his death.

During his first visit to her, Goneril picks an argument with Lear. The king has employed a new servant, unaware that it is Kent in disguise, and he also enjoys the services of his professional Fool, who with the particular license accorded to him points out the old king's foolishness in handing everything over to his daughters. When the inevitable confrontation with Goneril occurs, she divests Lear of half his retinue, and feeling the sharp pain of filial rejection he and his followers leave abruptly in the false expectation of better treatment by Regan.

Forewarned by Goneril, however, Regan and Cornwall leave to visit Gloucester in order to avoid Lear's arrival at their own palace. When Lear catches up with them, he finds to his annoyance that his servant Kent has, with some justification, been put in the stocks after a disagreement with Goneril's trusty servant Oswald. A dramatic scene ensues during which, in a magnificent double act, Goneril and Regan assert their power over Lear, divest him of his entourage, and cast him out helpless into a brewing storm. This concerted show of "filial ingratitude" begins to upset the balance of Lear's already disturbed mind.

Lear, Kent and the Fool find themselves out on the stormy heath without shelter. In his growing madness Lear challenges the elements to do their worst, seemingly oblivious to physical onslaught because of the tempest raging in his mind. Tormented by his daughters' actions, he sees everything in terms of his own recent experiences, and the storm as conspiring with his daughters against him. He shouts at the elements, revealing his own preoccupations, while the Fool tries to console him with humour ("labours to outjest his heart-struck injuries"). Kent finds them shelter in a hovel, where they discover Edgar, disguised as the lunatic Poor Tom o'Bedlam – hiding from search parties set after him as a result of his brother's treachery. So we have, at the core of the play, the genuinely mad Lear, the professional madman, and Edgar pretending to be mad. Their combined incongruity, and the way their dialogue bounces off each other with implied rather than direct responses, create a powerful vision of human struggle in a hostile world gone mad, a struggle impotent against the random forces of nature.

Meanwhile, unhappy about Lear's treatment, Gloucester makes the mistake of telling Edmund of his loyalty to the king, and that he is going out into the storm, against orders, to help him; he also reveals his secret knowledge of a French invasion to rescue Lear, whose death is now sought by Goneril and Regan. To further his own position, Edmund tells Cornwall and Regan of his father's "treason".

Gloucester finds Lear in his hovel, warns them of pursuit and the plot against his life, and so that they might escape provides them with urgent transport to Dover where Cordelia is waiting with the French army. On returning to his castle, he is apprehended and his eyes gouged out by Cornwall (with Regan as willing accomplice) as punishment for treason – though not before one of Gloucester's faithful servants has mortally wounded Cornwall in abhorrence at this cruelty. Regan kills the servant, informs the now blind Gloucester of Edmund's betrayal, and suggests that he "smell" his way to Dover.

CONTINUED...

With the storm over, Poor Tom discovers his father being led by an old retainer and, without revealing his true identity, takes over as his guide to Dover. Gloucester's unstated purpose is to jump off the cliff when he gets there.

The plot thickens. Goneril openly states her desire for Edmund, denigrating her husband in the process. Albany then enters, strongly criticising Goneril for her part in the heartless treatment of Lear. Goneril, who wears the trousers, taunts him. When they then learn of the events at Gloucester's house, Albany's sympathies are clearly with Gloucester and the king.

The king of France has returned home on urgent business, leaving Cordelia with his army under charge of a deputy. She is moved to great pity on hearing from Kent of her father's treatment, and holds no grudge against him for his behaviour towards her.

Whilst both sides prepare for battle, Regan, having recently committed adultery with Edmund, jealously asks Oswald to show her a letter to him from Goneril. He refuses, notwithstanding the recently widowed Regan's claim to be a more suitable spouse for Edmund than her married sister. She sees no reason for a period of mourning ("my lord is dead; Edmund and I have talked"). She also suggests that Oswald might usefully kill Gloucester should he happen to come across him.

Having reached the cliff at Dover, Edgar foils his father's planned suicide by pretending to lead him to the edge and letting him "jump". Not fully in control of his faculties, and inclined to belief in the supernatural, Gloucester swallows Edgar's story that he was led to the top by a demon but has miraculously survived the fall.

Gloucester and Edgar by chance now meet Lear who, having escaped his attendants, in his madness wears a crown of wild flowers. Gloucester recognises his voice, but before the king recognises him, he subjects them to a concentrated prattle of nonetheless penetrating observations. His madness is now less violent than during the tempest, though deeper. Observing this, Gloucester yearns for the release from pain and suffering which madness affords. When his attendants finally catch up with him, Lear runs off pursued, jabbering like a child.

Edgar and Gloucester are then accosted by Oswald, intent upon Regan's murderous instructions. He underestimates Edgar, who is dressed as a peasant, and in the ensuing sword-fight with him is killed. Edgar discovers a letter from Goneril to Edmund on the body, plotting the death of Albany, which he decides to pass on to the intended victim.

Near Dover, Cordelia thanks Kent for his brave care of her father who, sleeping, is brought in to be woken by her. In his disoriented state he thinks he has died and that she is a "soul in bliss", but as he comes round a touching reconciliation scene develops between the two.

Elsewhere, and with battle about to begin, Regan asks Edmund whether he has slept with Goneril, and we can surmise that his denials are untruthful. Albany now enters with Goneril, at which point the sisters' open rivalry for Edmund becomes evident. Edgar appears, still disguised, and privately hands Goneril's incriminating letter to the duke, saying that in response to a trumpet call after the battle he will produce a champion to uphold in combat the accusations arising from that letter against (the audience knows) Edmund.

Edmund privately considers his promises to both sisters, and plans the death of Lear and Cordelia in the event of an English victory. The English are indeed victorious, and Lear and Cordelia taken prisoner. Edmund coerces a reluctant captain to go and hang Cordelia in prison, and Albany, by now aware of the plot against his life, begins to come into his own, charging Edmund with capital treason, and throwing down his gauntlet to challenge him. Regan is carried off ill, poisoned by Goneril, and the challenge is accepted, but at the third trumpet blast the disguised Edgar arrives to uphold the challenge himself, mortally wounding Edmund in the ensuing fight. Goneril runs off, her plot having been revealed, and on learning the identity of his vanquisher, Edmund undergoes a deathbed admission of his crimes.

Edgar explains how their father has just died, happy to be reconciled with his son, at which point we learn that Goneril has admitted to poisoning Regan and then taken her own life. Kent enters to bid farewell to his king, and now Edmund admits he has ordered the deaths of Lear and Cordelia. Help arrives too late, and Lear enters carrying her body, having killed the soldier who hanged her. He recognises Kent, but his apprehension of all but his daughter's death is vague. This has all been too much for him, and he dies still holding Cordelia.

Albany tries to tidy up by suggesting that Kent and Edgar should jointly rule the kingdom, but Kent reveals he has not long to live so the burden falls on Edgar. There is no sense of a new and hopeful beginning.

NOTES

ACT
1

ACT 1, SC. 1 (308 lines)

King Lear's palace.

The Earls of Kent and Gloucester, long in the service of King Lear, discuss his relative favourtism towards his two sons-in-law, the Dukes of Albany and Cornwall. Gloucester introduces to Kent his own illegitimate son, the handsome Edmund, whom he loves as much as his legitimate elder son, Edgar.

A fanfare announces the arrival of Lear, his youngest daughter, Cordelia, and his two elder daughters, Goneril and Regan, together with their husbands the Dukes. Gloucester is ordered to attend on the Duke of Burgundy and the King of France, rival suitors for the hand of Cordelia.

Lear reveals that he intends to divide his kingdom among his daughters and pass on his responsibilities to them and their husbands **(Q1)**. This is followed by a surprising request for each of his daughters to tell him in turn, in front of the whole court, how much she loves him **(Q2)**, with the implication that their responses will influence their share.

NOTES

QUOTES FROM ACT 1, SC. 1:

1 **LEAR**

Meantime we shall express our darker purpose.
Give me the map there. Know that we have divided
In three our kingdom; and 'tis our fast intent
To shake all cares and business from our age,
Conferring them on younger strengths, while we
Unburdened crawl toward death. (35 − 40)

2 **LEAR**

Tell me, my daughters −
Since now we will divest us both of rule,
Interest of territory, cares of state −
Which of you shall we say doth love us most. (48 − 51)

Goneril, the first to go, plays the game **(Q3)** as does Regan **(Q4)**, and both are duly rewarded for their performances. Cordelia, her father's favourite **(Q5)**, refuses to participate in this charade, so her answer disappoints the vain and delusional king **(Q6)**, even though she points out the obvious insincerity in her sisters' responses **(Q7)**. Lear completely misinterprets Cordelia's words **(Q8)** and overreacts **(Q9)**, shocking all right-minded observers.

NƆTES

3 GONERIL
Sir, I do love you more than word can wield the matter (55)

4 REGAN
Sir, I am made of that self mettle as my sister (69)

And I find I am alone felicitate
In your dear highness' love. (75 — 6)

5 LEAR
                    ...what can you say to draw
A third more opulent than your sisters? Speak. (85 — 6)

6 CORDELIA
Nothing, my lord. (87)
LEAR
How, nothing will come of nothing. Speak again. (90)
CORDELIA
                    I love your majesty
According to my bond, no more nor less. (92 — 3)

7 CORDELIA
Why have my sisters husbands, if they say
They love you all? (99 — 100)

8 LEAR
So young and so untender?
CORDELIA
So young, my lord, and true. (107 — 8)

9 LEAR
Here I disclaim all my paternal care,
Propinquity and property of blood
And as a stranger to my heart and me
Hold thee from this for ever. (114 — 17)

The brave and honourable Kent tries to interject, but Lear, somewhat vaingloriously, silences him **(Q10)**. Stunned into inaction by his unwarranted rejection of Cordelia **(Q11)**, his attendants do not at first respond to his command to fetch France and Burgundy. Disinheriting Cordelia, he divests himself of all property and office **(Q12)**, dividing his kingdom between Albany and Cornwall, in the mistaken belief that he can retain the trappings of kingship (including a retinue of 100 knights) without any responsibility **(Q13)**.

This is all too much for Kent, who interjects again. Undeterred by Lear's implicit threat **(Q14)**, and at the risk of his life, he tells him exactly what he thinks **(Q15)**. When Lear's patience cracks, he is banished, and so years of loyalty are cast aside by the king in a rash moment of anger. As with Cordelia, Kent's honesty is misinterpreted as "pride". Kent is given five days, on pain of death, to leave the country. He departs, wishing Cordelia well, and expressing a skeptical hope to Goneril and Regan that their deeds will match their words.

NOTES

10 LEAR

Peace, Kent,
Come not between the dragon and his wrath! (122 — 3)

11 LEAR

[to Cordelia] Hence and avoid my sight.
So be my grave my peace, as here I give
Her father's heart from her. (125 — 7)

12 LEAR

I do invest you jointly with my power,
Pre-eminence and all the large effects
That troop with majesty. (131 — 3)

13 LEAR

...only we shall retain
The name, and all th'addition to a king (136 — 7)

14 LEAR

The bow is bent and drawn; make from the shaft. (144)

15 KENT

...be Kent unmannerly
When Lear is mad. What wouldst thou do, old man?
Think'st thou that duty shall have dread to speak,
When power to flattery bows? To plainness honour's bound
When majesty falls to folly. (146 — 50)

Gloucester brings in France and Burgundy; the latter is interested in Cordelia only if she comes complete with the promised dowry. France, who is not mercenary, cannot believe that Cordelia could really have done anything so gross as to deserve such reversal in her father's affection in so short a time **(Q16)**. As a point of honour, Cordelia wishes to make it clear that Lear's displeasure has not been caused by scandalous behaviour on her part, but (as all but Lear can see) by her refusal to indulge in smooth-talking hypocrisy **(Q17)** and to pretend to be what she is not purely for personal advantage **(Q18)** – but in vain, as the king rejects her in terms which are painfully unjust **(Q19)**.

France declares his love for Cordelia **(Q20)** and asks her to be his queen. Lear cannot refrain from a parting insult to his daughter **(Q21)**, who delivers a controlled but unfriendly farewell to her unrepentant sisters. Left on their own, Goneril and Regan comment upon their father's lack of judgement and unreasonable behaviour **(Q22)**, and not without good reason fear that they might themselves become the objects of similarly unpredictable behaviour. They therefore resolve to act together to prevent it.

NOTES

16 FRANCE

...which to believe of her
Must be a faith that reason without miracle
Should never plant in me. (222 — 4)

17 CORDELIA

If for I want that glib and oily art
To speak and purpose not... (227 — 7)

18 CORDELIA

But even for want of that for which I am richer,
A still soliciting eye and such a tongue
That I am glad I have not... (232 — 4)

19 LEAR

Go to, go to, better thou
Hadst not been born than not to have pleased me better. (235 — 6)

20 FRANCE

Fairest Cordelia, thou art most rich being poor,
Most choice forsaken and most loved despised (252 — 3)

21 LEAR

Thou hast her, France; let her be thine, for we
Have no such daughter, not shall ever see
That face of hers again. (264 — 6)

22 GONERIL

He always loved our sister most, and with what poor judgement
he hath now cast her off appears too grossly. (292 — 3)

ACT 1, SC. 2 (181 lines)

The Earl of Gloucester's castle.

If we were wondering at the beginning of the first scene how Edmund felt about the discussion between his father and Kent of his illegitimacy, all is now revealed – and already we have a clear idea of those who represent good and bad in the play. Edmund believes in the law of the jungle rather than civilized custom **(Q1)**, and therefore sees no reason why being a bastard **(Q2)** should prevent him from receiving his father's inheritance instead of Edgar **(Q3)**. He has fabricated a letter from Edgar, as part of a plot to bring about his downfall. **(Q4)**

Gloucester, shocked by recent events, comes in as Edmund pretends to pocket the letter hurriedly. He eventually hands it to his father with feigned reluctance. The forged letter expresses Edgar's supposed impatience at the power the old have over the young **(Q5)**, and suggests to Edmund the benefits of murdering their father **(Q6)**. Gloucester is too quick to believe ill of Edgar, setting aside in the heat of the moment (as did Lear with Cordelia) the positive characteristics which as his father he must have known Edgar to possess. Edmund is a smooth performer, masterfully hypocritical **(Q7)**, and Gloucester leaves it to Edmund to "prove" his brother's true intentions. However, supported by what he believes to be astrological portents, he has in effect already made up his mind as to Edgar's guilt **(Q8)**.

NOTES

_____

_____

_____

_____

_____

_____

_____

_____

_____

_____

_____

QUOTES FROM ACT 1, SC. 2:

1 EDMUND
Thou, nature, art my goddess; to thy law
My services are bound. (1—2)

2 EDMUND
Why bastard? Wherefore base?
When my dimensions are as well compact,
My mind as generous and my shape as true
As honest madam's issue? (6—9)

3 EDMUND
Well, then,
Legitimate Edgar, I must have your land. (15—16)

4 EDMUND
...if this letter speed
And my invention thrive, Edmund the base
Shall top the legitimate. (19—21)

5 GLOUCESTER *(Reads)*
...the oppression of aged tyranny, who sways not as it hath power,
but as it is suffered. (49—51)

6 GLOUCESTER *(Reads)*
If our father should sleep till I waked him, you should enjoy half
His revenue for ever and live the beloved of your brother. (52—4)

7 EDMUND
...suspend your indignation against my brother till you can derive from
him better testimony of his intent (80—1)

8 GLOUCESTER
Find out this villain, Edmund; it shall lose thee nothing. (114—15)

Edmund by contrast has no time for astrology **(Q9)**, believing that we are as we are and that we control our own fortunes. After Gloucester leaves, his brother comes back and, as if he knows something that Edgar does not, Edmund asks him if he has in any way offended their father, who is extremely angry with him. He advises Edgar to arm himself and to hide in his (Edmund's) lodgings. Edgar leaves, and Edmund chuckles at how easy it has been to use his father's and brother's innocence and finer qualities as the means of deceiving them **(Q10)**. For him, the ends justify the means **(Q11)**.

NOTES

9 EDMUND

This is the excellent foppery of the world, that when we are sick in fortune, often the surfeits of our own behavior, we make guilty of our disasters the sun, the moon and the stars (118 — 21)

10 EDMUND

A credulous father and a brother noble,
Whose nature is so far from doing harms
That he suspects none – on whose foolish honesty
My practices ride easy. (177 — 181)

11 EDMUND

All with me's meet that I can fashion fit. (182)

ACT 1, SC. 3 (27 lines)

The Duke of Albany's palace.

Spoiling for a fight with her father **(Q1)**, Goneril hears from her steward Oswald that Lear has struck one of her staff for criticizing his professional Fool. She instructs him to treat the king and his retinue with less than the normal courtesies when he returns from hunting, and she wishes to bring the issue to a head because he constantly criticizes her, and because his knights are behaving badly. She despises her father, in front of Oswald, for wishing to retain the privileges of kingship without the responsibilities that go with them **(Q2)**, and decides to write to Regan to ensure that they are at one on this issue.

NOTES

QUOTES FROM ACT 1, SC. 3:

1 **GONERIL**
By day and night he wrongs me. Every hour
He flashes into one gross crime or other
That sets us all at odds. (4 − 6)

2 **GONERIL**
                                    Idle old man,
That still would manage those authorities
That he hath given away. (17 − 19)

ACT 1, SC. 4 (344 lines)

A hall in the same.

The banished Kent, in lowly disguise and having made his way to Goneril's residence, resolves to take care of his master. Lear returns from hunting, in holiday mood, treating the house as his own, and Kent manages to inveigle himself into his service. One of the knights indicates to Lear that the standard of hospitality shown towards the king and his retinue is not what it was **(Q1)**. Shortly after, Oswald enters and, following Goneril's orders, shows disrespect towards the king, who strikes him, whereupon Kent earns his master's approval by sending him sprawling.

The Fool enters. He occupies a special position vis-à-vis the king in that he is permitted, up to a point, to make pertinent and even insulting comments under the mask of humour. It is clear that he is fond of Cordelia but not her sisters. He immediately implies to Kent that he is a fool for following the king in his now diminished position, and tells Lear he is a fool for giving everything to his daughters **(Q2 & 3)**. The Fool is no fool.

Oswald's treatment has given Goneril her excuse to complain to her father, and she duly comes to make as much as she can out of whatever legitimate grievance she might have. The Fool's perceptive comments antagonize her **(Q4)**. Lear, conscious always of the respect he feels is owed to him, also reacts with a degree of sarcasm and facetiousness guaranteed to inflame the situation, and plays into her hands by giving her the excuse to be blunt **(Q5)** and to criticize the riotous behaviour of his knights. Starting to exert her authority, there is an underlying threat in her request that he should reduce his retinue **(Q6)**.

NOTES

QUOTES FROM ACT 1, SC. 4:

1. **KNIGHT**
My lord, I know not what the matter is, but to my judgement your highness is not entertained with that ceremonious affection as you were wont. (55 – 7)

2. **LEAR**
Doest thou call me fool, boy?
FOOL
All thy other titles thou hast given away;
that thou wast born with
KENT
This is not altogether fool, my lord. (141 – 44)

3. **FOOL**
Thou hadst little wit in thy bald crown when thou gav'st thy golden one away. (155 – 56)

4. **FOOL**
For you know, nuncle,
The hedge-sparrow fed the cuckoo so long
That it's had it head bit off by it young. (205 – 7)

5. **GONERIL**
As you are old and reverend, should be wise. (231)

6. **GONERIL**
           Be then desired
By her that else will take the things she begs,
A little to disquantity your train. (238 – 40)

Lear reacts badly, sending insults flying ("Degenerate bastard" and "Detested kite, thou liest") in the face of which, for the moment at least, Goneril may seem more reasonable **(Q7)**, and certainly more in control of her emotions. Albany enters in the middle of the row, to witness Lear's frenzied overreaction, uncharitable even under the circumstances **(Q8 & Q9)**. His short fuse is reminiscent of his angry response to Cordelia in the first scene. He leaves in a huff, with Goneril unaffected by his ranting and raving **(Q10)**, and when he returns on discovering that his retinue has been halved, he becomes even more emotional and offensive **(Q11)**. Completely outmanoeuvred by Goneril, his misguided assumption that Regan will take his side is, despite our sympathies, a feeble thing to hear **(Q12)**.

After Lear's departure, her brief discussion with Albany shows that Goneril wears the trousers in their relationship. She justifies her actions by saying that Lear's retinue presented a threat of force against them, which Albany questions **(Q13)**. She sends Oswald with a letter informing Regan what has happened.

NOTES

7. GONERIL
You strike my people, and your disordered rabble
Make servants of their betters. (247—8)

8. LEAR
Hear, Nature, hear, dear goddess, hear:
Suspend thy purpose if thou didst intend
To make this creature fruitful. (267—69)

9. LEAR
How sharper than a serpent's tooth it is
To have a thankless child. (280—1)

10. GONERIL
But let his disposition have that scope
As dotage gives it. (284—5)

11. LEAR
Blasts and fogs upon thee!
Th'untented woundings of a father's curse
Pierce every sense about thee. (291—3)

12. LEAR
Ha? Let it be so. I have another daughter,
Who I am sure is kind and comfortable:
When she shall hear this of thee with her nails
She'll flay thy wolvish visage. (297—300)

13. ALBANY
Well, you may fear too far.
GONERIL
Safer than trust too far. (321—2)

ACT 1, SC. 5 (50 lines)

Court before the same.

Lear sends Kent with letters to Regan and Gloucester, telling him to be swift in his delivery so that he himself does not arrive before his communication. Then, alone in the company of the Fool, his surfacing regrets (probably at his treatment of Cordelia) distract him from the Fool's observations about his poor judgement in visiting Regan and thinking that she will be any different from her sister. Distracted as Lear is, their "conversation" is two separate monologues rather than a dialogue, and we see signs of his emerging madness **(Q1)**.

NOTES

QUOTES FROM ACT 1, SC. 5:

1 **FOOL**
Thou shouldst not have been old till thou hadst been wise.
LEAR
O let me not be mad, not mad, sweet heaven! I would not be mad.
Keep me in temper, I would not be mad. (41—5)

NOTES

ACT
2

ACT 2, SC.1 (131 lines)

Gloucester's castle.

Curan, a member of Gloucester's household, tells Edmund that Cornwall and Regan will arrive tonight, and asks if he has heard the rumours of strife between Albany and Cornwall. Edmund quickly sees how the upcoming royal presence might work to his advantage; he calls Edgar and, continuing his deception, tells him that his whereabouts has been discovered and asks him if he has not said anything against the two dukes. He thereby persuades Edgar that he must leave in haste, and stages a mock sword-fight between the two of them **(Q1)** in order to allow Edgar to "escape". This serves the dual purpose of convincing Edgar of his earnest support and persuading Gloucester, with the help of a self-inflicted wound **(Q2)**, of Edgar's villainy and his own loyalty in opposing such a plan.

The old earl falls for it completely, and says that, once apprehended, Edgar should be killed. Edmund then preempts and undermines any truthful argument that his brother might put forward once captured, by falsely reporting what Edgar said to him. Edmund's masterful deception reinforces Gloucester's willingness to believe the worst of his elder son.

As Cornwall's arrival is announced, he gives Edmund assurance that he rather than Edgar will inherit **(Q3)**, though we suspect that Edmund may not be prepared to wait that long. Cornwall and Regan, having been taken in by the false stories about Edgar (who, it now appears, is Lear's godson), and therefore impressed by Edmund, grant Gloucester whatever authority he needs to apprehend his son **(Q4)**. Edmund pledges his allegiance to Cornwall **(Q5)**, an unpleasant pact incongruously sealed with honourable words.

Regan now explains that the reason for their untimely visit is to seek Gloucester's advice on matters relating to Lear and Goneril, but also perhaps (if Curan's rumours about pending conflict between Albany and Cornwall are true) to get Gloucester on their side. In an ironic echo of Edmund's pledge of service to Cornwall, Gloucester, more naïvely pledges his support to Regan, "I serve you, madam" **(line 130)**.

QUOTES FROM ACT 2, SC. 1:

1 **EDMUND**
In cunning I must draw my sword upon you. (30)

2 **EDMUND**
Some blood drawn on me would beget opinion
Of my more fierce endeavour. [Cuts his arm] (34—5)

3 **GLOUCESTER**
Loyal and natural boy, I'll work the means
To make thee capable. (84—5)

4 **CORNWALL**
                    ...make your own purpose
How in my strength you please. For you, Edmund,
Whose virtue and obedience doth this instant
So much commend itself, you shall be ours.
Natures of such deep trust we shall much need. (112—16)

5 **EDMUND**
I shall serve you, sir, truly, however else. (118)

NOTES

ACT 2, SC.2 (499 lines)

Before Gloucester's castle.

A long and complex scene, which begins with Kent and Oswald arriving at Gloucester's castle before daybreak, having come there from delivering their separate messages to Regan. We already know from **1.iv** that Kent does not like Oswald, but his unrestrained antipathy here seems like yet another overreaction. His fluent insults stem in part from the difference in rank between them which Kent cannot of course reveal **(Q1)**. He tries to provoke the startled Oswald into a swordfight, which is interrupted by the arrival of Edmund, Cornwall, Regan and Gloucester. To these newcomers Kent's behaviour appears unreasonable, and this is compounded by his lack of respect towards Cornwall in particular **(Q2 & Q3)**. He certainly asks for trouble, as he did in the opening scene with Lear.

Cornwall, who is no fool, is not impressed with the protective cover of plain speaking behind which Kent uncompromisingly seeks to hide **(Q4)**. After a final insult which simply cannot be ignored, and Oswald's account of the affair, Cornwall orders him to be put in the stocks until noon – a punishment which Regan extends until the following morning. Such a punishment is, however, deemed inappropriate for a servant of the king, and will upset Lear when he finds out **(Q5)**.

Unrepentant, Cornwall and Regan leave Gloucester with Kent, and we have to accept that, despite the two earls' familiarity with each other, Kent's disguise remains impenetrable. Gloucester speaks to him as an equal, unhappy with Cornwall's treatment of him, and promises to intercede on his behalf, but Kent tells him not to bother. Left on his own, Kent reads a letter from Cordelia in which she promises to find a way of redressing the wrongs which have occurred. He then sleeps.

NOTES

QUOTES FROM ACT 2, SC. 2:

1 KENT

...art nothing but the composition of a knave, beggar, coward, pander and the son and heir of a mongrel bitch; one whom I will beat into clamorous whining if thou deniest the least syllable of thy addition.

OSWALD

Why, what a monstrous fellow art thou, thus to rail on one that is neither known of thee, nor knows thee! (20 — 6)

2 CORNWALL

Peace, sirrah. You beastly knave, know you no reverence?

KENT

Yes, sir, but anger hath a privilege.

CORNWALL

Why art thou angry?

KENT

That such a slave as this should wear a sword,
That wears no honesty. (66 — 71)

3 KENT

Sir, 'tis my occupation to be plain:
I have seen better faces in my time
Than stands on any shoulder that I see
Before me at this instant. (90 — 3)

4 CORNWALL

             He cannot flatter, he:
An honest mind and plain, he must speak truth;
An they will take it, so; if not, he's plain.
These kind of knaves I know. (96 — 9)

5 GLOUCESTER

The King, his master, needs must take it ill
That he, so slightly valued in his messenger,
Should have him thus restrained. (143 — 5)

Edgar, fresh from his narrow escape, resolves to adopt his own disguise in the form of a beggar **(Q6)**. Like Lear, he is to face the elements unprotected **(Q7)**, and names himself Poor Tom **(Q8)**.

Lear enters with his Fool and one of his knights, naïvely wondering why Cornwall and Regan were not at home to greet his arrival, and why they did not return his messenger. They then stumble upon Kent in the stocks, and at first Lear refuses to believe that his daughter and son-in-law could have so disregarded his status as the king's messenger as to have placed him there **(Q9)**. From Kent's one-sided explanation, we learn that when he arrived at Regan's house the previous night with Lear's message, the hated Oswald was given precedence over him. It was Goneril's message that caused them to leave in haste, and resulted in Kent being treated with disfavour and made to wait at Gloucester's residence until they were ready to respond.

Kent claims to have been punished for launching into Oswald again, omitting to mention his impertinence to Cornwall. Lear feels physically ill at this, and leaves to find Regan. A knight who had accompanied Lear wisely asks Kent if there's nothing more to his story **(Q10)**, which he untruthfully denies. The Fool criticises Kent for following a master in the process of his downfall **(Q11)**, but at the same time maintains that loyalty is more important than the wisdom of self-preservation **(Q12)**.

Meanwhile Lear is surprised to learn from Gloucester that Regan and Cornwall are unwilling to speak to him, but the sight of Kent in the stocks spurs him on to insist. They eventually appear, at which point Kent is set free. Lear starts to tell Regan about Goneril's treatment of him, not expecting to hear Regan to support her sister **(Q13)**. Having been forewarned by Goneril's message, she goes on to say bluntly that old age has caused him to lose his judgement, and that he should return to Goneril and apologise. The scene is therefore developing into a logical continuation of the exertion of power over him begun by Goneril in **1.iv**. Lear again overreacts with extreme insults towards Goneril which do not help his cause. He then tries to flatter Regan by telling her she could never act as harshly as Goneril. Everything he says in this speech turns out to be wrong, either through flattery or misjudgement **(Q14)**.

6 EDGAR
While I may scape
I will preserve myself, and am bethought
To take the basest and most poorest shape
That ever penury in contempt of man
Brought near to beast. (176 – 80)

7 EDGAR
And with presented nakedness outface
The winds and persecutions of the sky. (182 – 3)

8 EDGAR
Poor Turlygood, poor Tom,
That's something yet: Edgar I nothing am. (191 – 2)

9 LEAR
They durst not do't:
They could not, would not do't – 'tis worse than murder
To do upon respect such violent outrage. (212 – 4)

10 KNIGHT
Made you no more offence but what you speak of?
KENT
None. (251 – 2)

11 FOOL
Let go thy hold when a great wheel runs down a hill
lest it break thy neck with following it. (261 – 2)

12 FOOL
But I will tarry, the fool will stay,
And let the wise man fly:
The knave turns fool that runs away,
The fool no knave perdy. (271 – 4)

13 REGAN
I pray you, sir, take patience. I have hope
You less know how to value her desert
Than she to scant her duty. (327 – 9)

14 LEAR
Thou better knowst
The offices of nature, bond of childhood,
Effects of courtesy, dues of gratitude. (366 – 8)

Lear asks who put his man in the stocks, but before he can be answered Oswald, and then Goneril appear; the sisters take each other by the hand in a gesture of support, much to Lear's surprise.

Their confidence and defiance show us that the cards are stacked against Lear **(Q15)**, who now learns that it was Cornwall who ordered Kent to be put in the stocks. But Lear can do nothing. The sisters begin a double-act which systematically strips Lear of all that remains to him, exposing the powerlessness which he has brought upon himself, and there is dramatic irony in his response to Regan's initial suggestion that he dismiss half his knights and return to Goneril **(Q16)**. Once more the strength of his overreaction plays into their hands **(Q17)**. It takes Lear a while to realise that his daughters are as one against him, despite which he is almost childishly out of touch with reality, still setting store by the wrong things **(Q18)**.

When Regan finally asks why he even needs one knight in his retinue, he says that human existence is not just about need **(Q19)**, and fades into impotent rage **(Q20)**.

Outside a storm begins, reflecting the tempest unfolding in Lear's mind. He leaves in frustration, rage and despair. Goneril is wholly unsympathetic, commenting that her father has brought this upon himself **(Q21)**. Despite Gloucester's objections, and usurping his authority in his own home, they shut Lear and his followers out of the castle and leave him to the ravages of the oncoming storm **(Q22)**.

NOTES

15 GONERIL
Why not by the hand, sir? How have I offended?
All's not offence that indiscretion finds
And dotage terms so. (384 − 6)

16 LEAR
No! Rather I abjure all roofs and choose
To wage against the enmity o'th'air... (397 − 8)

17 LEAR
                    Thou art a boil,
A plague sore, or embossed carbuncle
In my corrupted blood. (412 − 4)

18 LEAR *[to Goneril]*
                    I'll go with thee;
Thy fifty yet doth double five and twenty,
And thou art twice her love. (271 − 4)

19 LEAR
O, reason not the need! Our basest beggars
Are in the poorest things superfluous;
Allow not nature more than nature needs,
Man's life is cheap as beast's. (453 − 6)

20 LEAR
                    No, you unnatural hags,
I will have such revenges on you both
That all the world shall − I will do such things −
What they are yet I know not, but they shall be
The terrors of the earth! (467 − 71)

21 GONERIL
'Tis his own blame; hath put himself from rest
And must needs taste his folly. (479 − 80)

22 REGAN
                    O sir, to willful men
The injuries that they themselves procure
Must be their schoolmasters. (492 − 4)

NOTES

ACT
3

ACT 3, SC.1 (50 lines)

A wood.

Outside in the storm Kent asks one of Lear's knights where the king is. He replies that he's out there battling the elements on this terrible night **(Q1)** with nobody but the Fool to give him solace **(Q2)**. Kent introduces an atmosphere of intrigue by confiding to the knight that there is secret enmity between Albany and Cornwall, and that he knows from spies placed by the king of France that trouble is brewing. This follows on from Cordelia's letter which Kent was reading in the stocks. He explains that he is a man of some status, and asks the knight to travel to Dover to inform Cordelia of her father's treatment. But first they must search for the king. Kent is doing his utmost to care for his helpless master.

ACT 3, SC.2 (96 lines)

Before Gloucester's castle. Kent in the stocks.

Lear, losing his mind, conducts a spirited monologue against the raging storm **(Q1 & Q2)**. Windswept and drenched to the skin, in an orgy of cataclysmic and sexual imagery he challenges nature to do its worst and drown the world in a second deluge. The loyal Fool, more in touch with surface reality, sees the folly of pitting oneself against the overwhelming power of nature **(Q3)**. There is no chance of imposing order on the world, but despite his follies, our sympathies are with Lear who, before succumbing to madness, begins to understand his true situation **(Q4)**. Kent finds them and gives us a sense of the terror of the storm.

Affected by his own unjust treatment, Lear suggests that the gods might use the storm to dispense retribution on those whose unseen crimes have escaped human justice. He sees himself as "a man More sinned against than sinning" **(lines 58 — 9)**.

Kent tries to persuade the king, bareheaded as he is, to take shelter in a nearby hovel whilst he returns to Gloucester's castle to try to persuade Cornwall and Regan to let them in. Lear, beginning perhaps to think about others, and mainly for the sake of the Fool, allows himself to be led to shelter; meanwhile the Fool addresses the audience with a nonsensical prophecy of the world turned upside down, presenting a contradictory picture of fantasy and reality, and inviting us to realise that no sense can be made of his words **(Q5)**, nor, by extension, of the situation in which they find themselves. In this world, common sense and order will never prevail.

QUOTES FROM ACT 3, SC. 1:

1 KNIGHT
Strives in his little world of man to outscorn
The to and fro conflicting wind and rain; (10 — 11)

2 KNIGHT
None but the fool, who labours to outjest
His heart-struck injuries. (16 — 17)

QUOTES FROM ACT 3, SC. 2:

1 LEAR
Blow winds and crack your cheeks! Rage, blow!
You cataracts and hurricanoes, spout
Til you have drenched out steeples, drowned the cocks! (1 — 3)

2 LEAR
　　　　　　　　　　And thou, all-shaking thunder,
Strike flat the thick rotundity o'the world,
Crack nature's moulds. All germens spill at once
That make ingrateful man! (6 — 9)

3 FOOL
　　　　　　　　　Here's a night that pities neither
wise men nor fools... (12 — 13)

4 LEAR
　　　　　　　Here I stand your slave,
A poor, infirm, weak and despised old man. (19 — 20)

5 FOOL
This prophecy shall Merlin make, for I live before his time. (95)

ACT 3, SC.3 (24 lines)

A heath.

Gloucester unwisely confesses to Edmund his loyalty to the king, and even more unwisely reveals the existence of a secret letter which explains how moves are underfoot to redress the wrongful treatment of Lear. He leaves to try to give some relief to his "old master", whereupon Edmund instantly resolves to tell all to Cornwall, and with callous irony justifies supplanting his father as Earl of Gloucester **(Q1)**.

NOTES

QUOTES FROM ACT 3, SC. 3:

1   EDMUND
This seems a fair deserving and must draw me
That which my father loses, no less than all.
The younger rises when the old doth fall. $(22-4)$

N➔TES

ACT 3, SC.4 (180 lines)

The heath. Before a hovel.

Lear's progression towards madness is not a straight line: moments of lucidity are interspersed with his child-like obsessions, such as his response "Wilt break my heart?" when Kent offers to guide him into the hovel to protect him from the raging storm. Lear claims hardly to feel the physical impact of the tempest, because there is worse inside his head **(Q1)**. He is, again, aware of his oncoming madness **(Q2)**.

After the Fool and Kent enter the hovel, he stays outside to kneel and pray, thinking properly for the first time of those less fortunate than himself. He realizes he should have done so before, and shared his superfluous possessions in the interests of a fairer world **(Q3)**. For the first time he is showing responsibility and compassion as a ruler – just when he no longer has the power to rule. Contributing to the tragedy of *King Lear* is the fact that most of the important lessons are learned too late.

This brief interlude is interrupted from within the hovel by Edgar, disguised as Poor Tom, blurting out nonsense much to the alarm of the Fool. As his mind slips further into madness, Lear projects his own recent experience onto Tom, asking him if it is his daughters who have brought him to this pass **(Q4)**. It is Tom/Edgar rather than the Fool who now begins to absorb Lear's attention.

Tom provides much of the dialogue in this scene, and his ramblings and references to country superstitions and evil spirits create a more disturbing level of nonsense than the Fool's professional humour, and it is sometimes difficult, in the atmosphere of chaos and tempest, to remember that Edgar is just pretending to be mad.

In fact, compared to Poor Tom, the Fool's comments make perfect sense **(Q5)**. Even Lear, in his reduced state, feels that the deranged, half-naked Tom is a deserving object of his pity, an example of man at the most basic, animal level, whose nakedness he wishes to imitate **(Q6)**. He is, however, prevented from stripping off, and there is irony in the fact that Lear's observations, reasonable as they seem, are based on a fallacy: poor mad Tom is neither poor nor mad – he is in fact Edgar, the perfectly sane son of an earl.

QUOTES FROM ACT 3, SC. 4:

1 LEAR
The body's delicate: this tempest in my mind
Doth from my senses take all feeling else,
Save what beats there, filial ingratitude. (12—14)

2 LEAR
Your old, kind father, whose frank heart gave you all –
O, that way madness lies, let me shun that;
No more of that. (20—22)

3 LEAR [Kneels]
Poor naked wretches, wheresoe'er you are,
That bide the pelting of this pitiless storm,
How shall your houseless heads and unfed sides,
Your looped and windowed raggedness, defend you
From seasons such as these? O, I have ta'en
Too little care of this. Take physic, pomp,
Expose thyself to feel what wretches feel,
That thou mayst shake the superflux to them
And show the heavens more just. (28—36)

4 EDGAR
Away, the foul fiend follows me. Through the
sharp hawthorn blows the cold wind. Humh, go to
thy cold bed and warm thee.
LEAR
Didst thou give all to thy two daughters? And art
thou come to this? (45—9)

5 EDGAR
Pillicock sat on Pillicock hill,
Alow, alow, loo, loo!
FOOL
This cold night will turn us all to fools and madmen. (75—7)

6 LEAR
                        Ha? Here's three on's
us are sophisticated; thou art the thing itself.
Unaccommodated man is no more but such a poor,
bare, forked animal as thou art. Off, off, you lendings:
come unbutton here. (103—7)

Gloucester now approaches on his mission of mercy carrying a torch, and of course fails to recognise his son Edgar in Poor Tom. He asks Lear to follow him to proper shelter **(Q7)** and sustenance. His mind slipping further, Lear wishes to talk first with his "philosopher" Poor Tom, whose words have impressed him. In the world turned upside down, Edgar's nonsense counts as wisdom.

Gloucester, speaking to Kent, compares his own unsettled state of mind with Lear's **(Q8)**. His conclusions, too, are based on a fallacy.

NOTES

7 *Go in with me. My duty cannot suffer*
T'obey in all your daughters' hard commands. (144−5)

8 **LEAR**
I am almost mad myself. I had a son,
Now outlawed from my blood; he sought my life. (162−4)
                    True to tell thee,
The grief hath crazed my wits. (165−6)

ACT 3, SC.5 (25 lines)

Gloucester's castle.

Cornwall, informed by Edmund that Gloucester is still loyal to the king, wants revenge. Ever the hypocrite, Edmund pretends that the conflict between his loyalty to his family and the higher call of duty causes him grievous pain **(Q1)**.

ACT 3, SC.6 (112 lines)

A chamber in a farmhouse adjoining the castle.

Unaware of Edmund's treachery, Gloucester leads Lear and the others to shelter. There is a brief moment of sanity when Kent thanks Gloucester for his kindness, and then we are launched into a conversation on three different levels of madness between Edgar, Lear and the Fool. Lear begins a mock trial of his daughters, much like a child's game of pretend, except that it incorporates legal terminology and adult vocabulary; combined with Tom's rhymes and irrelevant comments, this game of pretend creates a strong sense of justice being farcical. The Fool plays along, whilst Lear is in earnest. Edgar, in an aside, confesses to finding this pitiful sight almost too much to bear **(Q1)**.

Kent tries to soothe his master, who eventually falls into a much-needed sleep. Gloucester returns with news that there is a plot to kill the king, so they must leave without delay. All exit but Edgar who, reverting to his true identity, soliloquises that his own pains now seem less having witnessed Lear's. He will mark time until events disprove the false opinions held about him.

NOTES

- -
- -
- -
- -
- -
- -
- -

QUOTES FROM ACT 3, SC. 5:

1 **EDMUND**
> *O heavens! That this treason*
> *were not, or I not the detector.* (12 – 13)

QUOTES FROM ACT 3, SC. 6:

1 **EDGAR**
> *My tears begin to take his part so much*
> *They mar my counterfeiting.* (59 – 60)

ACT 3, SC.7 (106 lines)

Gloucester's castle.

A nasty scene which shows Cornwall and Regan in their true colours. Cornwall knows from Edmund that the French army has landed, so asks Goneril to convey this information to her husband Albany. He then orders the "traitor" Gloucester to be brought to him; Goneril and Regan are keen to join in the fun **(Q1)**. Edmund is despatched with Goneril so as not to have to witness his father's punishment. To make matters worse for Gloucester, Cornwall now learns from Oswald that he helped the king and three dozen of his knights escape towards Dover to meet up with Cordelia's French forces.

Though he knows he does not have authority to kill Gloucester, Cornwall looks forward to his revenge **(Q2)**. The old man, bound to a chair, is brought in and immediately abused by Cornwall and Regan. Under questioning he defiantly admits he helped the king escape from the cruelty of his daughters to Dover **(Q3)**. There is dramatic irony in these words as Cornwall now plucks out one of his eyes to the encouragement of Regan. This cruelty provokes one of Gloucester's servants to fight Cornwall and wound him – fatally, as it turns out – before he is himself stabbed from behind by Regan and killed.

The wounded duke plucks out Gloucester's other eye, and in his agony the old man calls upon Edmund *in absentia* to exact revenge. Regan takes pleasure in telling him that it was Edmund who betrayed him **(Q4)**, and so he realises his injustice towards Edgar **(Q5)**. She orders a servant to kick him out of his own house **(Q6)**, and it then becomes clear that Cornwall is badly wounded. The remaining servants who witnessed this terrible scene are shocked, and resolve to do what they can to help their blinded master.

NƎTES

_ _

_ _

_ _

_ _

_ _

_ _

QUOTES FROM ACT 3, SC. 7:

1   **REGAN**
Hang him instantly!
GONERIL
Pluck out his eyes!
CORNWALL
Leave him to my displeasure. (4 — 6)

2   **CORNWALL**
Though well we may not pass upon his life
Without the form of justice, yet our power
Shall do a courtesy to our wrath, which men
May blame but not control. (24 — 7)

3   **REGAN**
Wherefore to Dover, sir?
GLOUCESTER
Because I would not see thy cruel nails
Pluck out his poor old eyes; nor thy fierce sister
In his anointed flesh stick boarish fangs. (54 — 57)

4   **REGAN**
Thou call'st on him that hates thee. It was he
That made the overture of thy treasons to us,
Who is too good to pity thee. (86 — 9)

5   **GLOUCESTER**
O my follies! Then Edgar was abused? (90)

6   **REGAN**
Go, thrust him out at gates and let him smell
His way to Dover. (93 — 4)

NOTES

ACT
4

ACT 4, SC.1 (83 lines)

The heath.

A short soliloquy from Edgar in which he states that he is still better off in his lowly guise, as things can only improve. He is immediately proved wrong in this by the appearance of his blind father led by an old retainer. Gloucester tells the old servant to leave him be, but the servant protests that he cannot see his way. Gloucester replies that he has nowhere to go, and that anyway he was "blind" (in the sense of lacking understanding) when he had eyes **(Q1)**. If he could only now touch Edgar, he would feel he had eyes again **(Q2)**, whereupon the old servant catches sight of poor mad Tom.

Edgar addresses his father, noticing his bleeding eye sockets, and lapses again into his role as madman when Gloucester asks if he knows the way to Dover. The servant objects that Gloucester is seeking to be led by a madman, but he is unconcerned **(Q3)**. The old earl offers him money and, in an echo of Lear's prayer at **3.iv.33—36**, he says that a man who lives an excessive and lustful life, defying the rules of heaven, blind and unfeeling to the plight of others, should feel heaven's power and redress the balance by distributing what is superfluous to him so that everyone has enough **(Q4)**.

He then asks Poor Tom, in exchange for a rich reward, to lead him to the edge of a cliff at Dover, from where he will require no further guidance.

NOTES

QUOTES FROM ACT 4, SC. 1:

1 GLOUCESTER
I have no way, and therefore want no eyes:
I stumbled when I saw. (20 — 21)

2 GLOUCESTER
Might I but live to see thee in my touch,
I'd say I had eyes again. (25 — 26)

3 GLOUCESTER
'Tis the time's plague when madmen lead the blind. (49)

4 GLOUCESTER
     Heavens deal so still!
Let the superfluous and lust-dieted man
That slaves your ordinance, that will not see
Because he does not feel, feel your power quickly:
So distribution should undo excess
And each man have enough. (69 — 74)

ACT 4, SC.2 (98 lines)

Before Albany's palace.

Goneril and Edmund have dropped the formalities, and arrive at Albany's house accompanied by Oswald, who reports that Albany is strangely changed and seemingly opposed to his wife's values **(Q1)**. Goneril dismisses this as a cowardly unwillingness to act expediently, and it becomes clear that she and Edmund have struck up an amorous accord.

In view of what she perceives as her husband's weakness, she believes she must take command of the situation herself **(Q2)**, and sends Edmund back to help Cornwall assemble his army, though not before giving him a love-token and a kiss, and making her disdain for Albany abundantly clear. As Edmund leaves she remarks to herself on the contrast between the two men **(Q3)**.

When Albany enters they immediately exchange insults **(Q4)**, as he criticizes her treatment of her father. His insults are strong **(Q5)** and she retorts in like kind **(Q6)**, so an argument is underway when a messenger interrupts to say that Cornwall has died of his wound and that, to Albany's horror, Gloucester's eyes have been put out. He hands Goneril a note from Regan which requires an urgent response. She does not reply immediately, more concerned that Regan, now free of her husband, may be up to no good alone with Edmund. Albany learns that Edmund has betrayed his father, and his sympathies are clearly with Gloucester **(Q7)**.

NOTES

QUOTES FROM ACT 4, SC. 2:

1 OSWALD

I told him of the army that was landed;
He smiled at it. I told him you were coming;
His answer was 'The worse'. Of Gloucester's treachery
And of the loyal service of his son,
When I informed him, he called me sot... (4 — 8)

2 GONERIL

I must change names at home and give the distaff
Into my husband's hands. (17 — 18)

3 GONERIL

O, the difference of man and man!
To thee a woman's services are due;
A fool usurps my bed. (26 — 28)

4 ALBANY

You are not worth the dust which the rude wind
Blows in your face. (31 — 32)

5 ALBANY

Tigers, not daughters... (41)

6 GONERIL

Milk-livered man... (51)
... that not knowst
Fools do those villains pity who are punished
Ere they have done their mischief. (54 — 56)

7 ALBANY

Gloucester, I live
To thank thee for the love thou showd'st the King
And to revenge thine eyes.. (95 — 97)

ACT 4, SC.3 (56 lines)

The French camp near Dover.

Kent, still in disguise, learns that the King of France has had to return home on urgent business, leaving one of his marshalls in charge of his army. A gentleman tells him that his letters to Cordelia about her father's treatment have touched her very deeply, so it is clear that she has forgiven Lear for his earlier folly **(Q1)**. Kent explains, however, that Lear, falling in and out of madness, cannot bring himself for shame to come face-to-face with Cordelia **(Q2)**, and sends the gentleman off to look after the king.

ACT 4, SC.4 (29 lines)

The same. A tent.

We see Cordelia for the first time since **1.i.** She is bemoaning Lear's madness **(Q1)**, and offers all her wealth to anyone who can cure him. She is told that what the king really needs is rest.

A messenger enters with news that the British forces are approaching, but Cordelia replies that they are already prepared for the attack. She explains that the king of France lent her his forces purely to right the wrongs done to her father, and not for territorial gains **(Q2)**.

ACT 4, SC.5 (43 lines)

Gloucester's castle.

Oswald has reached Regan and explains that her sister, rather than Albany, has military matters under control ("your sister is the better soldier"). Regan says it was a mistake not to have killed Gloucester, because of the general sympathy he might now generate, and then tries to persuade Oswald to show her a letter he is carrying from Goneril to Edmund. Her speech is the first indication that Goneril's jealousy over Edmund is well-founded. She speaks plainly to Oswald, saying that it is she who would make a more appropriate wife for Edmund – her husband now being dead – and implies that she and Edmund have slept together **(Q1)**.

Regan then suggests that he should kill Gloucester at the first opportunity, to which he agrees.

QUOTES FROM ACT 4, SC. 3:

1 GENTLEMAN

Those happy smilets
That played on her ripe lip seemed not to know
What guests were in her eyes, which parted thence
As pearls from diamonds dropped. (19 – 22)

2 KENT

A sovereign shame so elbows him. His own unkindness
That stripped her from his benediction... (43 – 44)
...these things sting
His mind so venomously that burning shame
Detains him from Cordelia. (46 – 48)

QUOTES FROM ACT 4, SC. 4:

1 CORDELIA

Alack, 'tis he. Why, he was met even now
As mad as the vexed sea, singing aloud,
Crowned with rank fumiter and furrow-weeds... (1 – 3)

2 CORDELIA

No blown ambition doth our arms incite,
But love, dear love, and our aged father's right. (27 – 28)

QUOTES FROM ACT 4, SC. 5:

1 REGAN

My lord is dead; Edmund and I have talked,
And more convenient is he for my hand
Than for your lady's. You may gather more. (33 – 35)

ACT 4, SC.6 (281 lines)

Fields near Dover.

Edgar, posing as a peasant, pretends to lead Gloucester to the edge of the cliff.
He speaks no longer as Tom, nor yet quite as Edgar **(Q1)**. His father gives him a
valuable jewel in return for guiding him, and prepares, as he thinks, to jump off a
cliff to his death. Edgar bids him farewell and explains, in an aside, that he hopes
this deception will cure his father of despair **(Q2)**. Gloucester offers a valedictory
prayer to the gods **(Q3)**, and then falls down – though obviously not very far.

The scene becomes surreal, dream-like, in part almost nightmarish – in
contrast to the realism that has gone before. Edgar is concerned that his father's
willingness to die may of itself cause his death **(Q4)**. Pretending to be yet
someone else, he speaks to him as if from the spot where he has "landed" down
below, saying that miraculously he is still alive, only his gossamer-like lightness
having saved him from death **(Q5)**.

Gloucester, at first dismayed by his survival **(Q6)**, is diverted by Edgar's
description of a strange, devil-like creature that he observed from below leading
him to the cliff-edge **(Q7)**. Gloucester's superstitious nature evidently permits
him to swallow this story, and the old man decides from now on to bear his
afflictions in accordance with divine will rather than try to end them by
suicide **(Q8)**.

NOTES

_____

_____

_____

_____

_____

_____

_____

_____

QUOTES FROM ACT 4, SC. 6:

1 EDGAR
*Come on, sir, here's the place. Stand still: how fearful
And dizzy 'tis to cast one's eyes so low.
The crows and choughs that wing the midway air
Show scarce as gross as beetles.* (11 – 14)

2 EDGAR *[aside]*
*Why I do trifle thus with his despair
Is done to cure it.* (33 – 34)

3 GLOUCESTER *[he kneels]*
                    *O you mighty gods,
This world I do renounce and in your sights
Shake patiently my great affliction off.* (34 – 36)

4 EDGAR *[aside]*
*And yet I know not how conceit may rob
The treasury of life when life itself
Yields to the theft.* (42 – 44)

5 EDGAR
*Hadst thou been aught but gossamer, feathers, air,
So many fathom down precipitating,
Thou'dst shivered like an egg...* (49 – 51)

6 GLOUCESTER
*Is wretchedness deprived that benefit
To end itself by death?* (61 – 62)

7 EDGAR
*As I stood here below methought his eyes
Were two full moons. He had a thousand noses,
Horns whelked and waved like the enraged sea.
It was some fiend.* (69 – 72)

8 GLOUCESTER
*I do remember now. Henceforth I'll bear
Affliction til it do cry out itself
'Enough, enough, and die.* (75 – 77)

Into this strange reverie comes Lear, crowned, as Cordelia earlier described, with flowers, and babbling away, apparently escaped from his attendants. He recounts, as if a child, his experience of the storm **(Q9)**. Gloucester, blind and confused, asks if it is not the king's voice. Lear has sufficient grasp of his surroundings to respond in the affirmative **(Q10)**, though his speech quickly moves to other preoccupations: subconsciously he alludes to Gloucester's own crime of adultery, saying that it should not be punished, because lechery is natural and universal **(Q11)**. Every living creature is at it: hypocrisy, lust and filth.

In his insanity, Lear's comments are stripped of the distorting restraints of convention, releasing a quality of innocent and objective truth which repeatedly, and often painfully, hits the bull's-eye. As if he had not heard Lear's tirade, Gloucester asks to kiss his hand, but the king responds on another level **(Q12)**. These different layers of consciousness on which the characters operate cause their comments to ricochet with alternative meanings, much as in **3.iv** and **3.vi**.

The conversation between the two old men shows long familiarity and shared pain, and exhibits a harmless disconnect from reality and an artless perspicacity which touch Edgar with great pity **(Q13)**. Lear's madness, though, has some method to it, and he aptly remarks on the topsy-turvy nature of justice **(Q14)**, against which privilege and wealth are an unfair protection **(Q15)**. As Edgar points out, Lear mixes nonsense with reason **(Q16)**. In a moment of clarity Lear recognises Gloucester **(Q17)**, before lapsing again into his own little world.

NOTES

_____

_____

_____

_____

_____

_____

_____

_____

9 LEAR

When the rain came to wet me once and the
wind to make me chatter; when the thunder would not
peace at my bidding, there I found 'em, there I smelt 'em out. (100 — 103)

10 LEAR

Ay, every inch a king.
When I do stare, see how the subject quakes. (106 — 7)

11 LEAR

The wren goes to't and the small gilded fly
Does lecher in my sight. Let copulation thrive... (111 — 12)

12 GLOUCESTER

O, let me kiss that hand!
LEAR
Let me wipe it first, it smells of mortality.
GLOUCESTER
O ruined piece of nature, this great world
Shall so wear out to naught. (128 — 131)

13 EDGAR [*aside*]

I would not take this from report: it is,
And my heart breaks at it. (137 — 38)

14 LEAR

Thou, rascal beadle, hold thy bloody hand;
Why dost thou lash that whore? Strip thine own back,
Thou hotly lusts to use her in that kind
For which thou whipp'st her. The usurer hangs the cozener. (156 — 59)

15 LEAR

Through tattered clothes great vices do appear;
Robes and furred gowns hide all. Plate sin with gold,
And the strong lance of justice hurtless breaks. (160 — 62)

16 EDGAR

O matter and impertinency mixed,
Reason in madness. (170 — 71)

17 LEAR

If thou wilt weep my fortunes, take my eyes.
I know thee well enough, thy name is Gloucester. (172 — 73)

Lear's attendants catch up with him and take hold of him. His admission of his own madness **(Q18)** is a good illustration of Edgar's description of his "reason in madness". He alternately thinks he is under arrest, or being attacked, and runs off prattling incoherently **(Q19)**.

Edgar now learns that battle is imminent. Having witnessed Lear in a worse state than him, Gloucester resolves, to Edgar's approval, not to try to take his own life again **(Q20)**.

Oswald chances upon them on his way back from Regan and, recognising Gloucester, threatens to kill him. However, he underestimates the protection afforded by Edgar, apparently just a peasant, and is mortally wounded in the ensuing sword-fight between them. Before he dies, he asks Edgar to give the letters he bears to "Edmund, Earl of Gloucester." Edgar's epitaph to Oswald is apt **(Q21)**. He learns from the letters of a plot by Goneril and Edmund to kill Albany and then marry **(Q22)**, so resolves to make Albany aware of it.

Gloucester rues his sanity, seeing madness as a comfort from distress **(Q23)**, and Edgar leads him towards a place of safety away from the approaching battle.

NOTES

18 LEAR

> Let me have surgeons,
> I am cut to the brains. (188 – 89)

19 GENTLEMAN

> A sight most pitiful in the meanest wretch,
> Past speaking of in a king. (200 – 1)

20 GLOUCESTER

> You ever gentle gods, take my breath from me;
> Let not my worser spirit tempt me again
> To die before you please. (213 – 15)

21 EDGAR

> ...a serviceable villain,
> As duteous to the vices of thy mistress
> As badness would desire. (247 – 49)

22 EDGAR

> A plot upon her virtuous husband's life
> And the exchange my brother. (267 – 68)

23 GLOUCESTER

> Better I were distract;
> So should my thoughts be severed from my griefs,
> And woes by wrong imagination lose
> The knowledge of themselves. (276 – 79)

ACT 4, SC.7 (96 lines)

A tent in the French camp. Lear on a bed asleep,

Cordelia thanks Kent for his help and care for her father. The gentleman tells her that it is time to wake the sleeping king, and asks that she be present. She is completely without resentment towards her father **(Q1)**, and full of pity for his ordeal during the storm **(Q2)**.

As her father awakens, Cordelia gently addresses him, and so begins their reconciliation. Slowly coming round, he supposes that he is dead, regarding Cordelia as a spirit in heaven and himself as damned and tormented **(Q3)**. Confused as to his whereabouts, and not yet recognising her, he could not be more different from the arrogant ruler of the opening scene, aware now of his faults and his uncertain mental state **(Q4)**.

At last recognising Cordelia, as well as his own guilt, he lays himself at her mercy **(Q5)** and is forgiven. He walks off arm in arm with her, whilst Kent and the gentleman discuss recent rumours and the forthcoming battle.

NOTES

QUOTES FROM ACT 4, SC. 7:

1 CORDELIA
O my dear father, restoration hang
Thy medicine on my lips, and let this kiss
Repair those violent harms that my two sisters
Have in thy reverence made. (26 — 29)

2 CORDELIA
                                    Mine enemy's dog
Though he had bit me should have stood that night
Against my fire. (36 — 38)

3 LEAR
You do me wrong to take me out o'the grave.
Thou art a soul in bliss, but I am bound
Upon a wheel of fire that mine own tears
Do scald. (45 — 48)

4 LEAR
I am a very foolish, fond old man,
Fourscore and upward, not an hour more nor less;
And to deal plainly
I fear I am not in my perfect mind.
Methinks I should know you and know this man,
Yet I am doubtful. (60 — 65)

5 LEAR
If you have poison for me, I will drink it.
I know you do not love me, for your sisters
Have, as I do remember, done me wrong.
You have some cause, they have not. (72 — 75)

NOTES

ACT
5

ACT 5, SC.1 (70 lines)

The British camp, near Dover.

Edmund sends someone to ask for clear battle directions from Albany, and it becomes clear to Regan that Oswald has gone missing. She then questions Edmund searchingly as to whether he has slept with Goneril **(Q1)**, which he flatly denies – just as she and Albany arrive. The Duke is in charge now that Cornwall is dead. He announces that although there may be good reasons for sympathizing with Lear and his supporters, the main question at issue is the French threat to British territory – to the frustration of Regan and Goneril who regard this as blindingly obvious **(Q2)**.

Over Edmund, though, they are not in agreement, and their jealousy surfaces as the three of them exit, leaving Albany to be approached privately by Edgar, still dressed as a peasant. Intent on making Albany aware of Goneril's and Edmund's plot against him, Edgar hands him the letter he found on Oswald's body. Edgar asks him, in the event of a British victory, to sound a trumpet, at which point he undertakes to produce a champion to uphold in combat the claims the letter makes. Albany agrees to read the letter, and Edgar leaves.

Edmund comes to inform Albany that the enemy is in sight and that haste is needed. Left on his own, Edmund admits that he is pledged to both sisters **(Q3)**, and decides that after the battle Goneril should find some means of disposing of Albany, so that he is free to dispose of Lear and Cordelia, rather than pardoning them as Albany would undoubtedly do. He must act expediently **(Q4)**.

ACT 5, SC.2 (12 lines)

A field between the two camps.

Edgar, still disguised as a peasant, stows his father in a safe place away from the battle. He returns in due course with the news that Lear's side (the French) has lost, and that the king and Cordelia have been taken prisoner. They are not safe where they are, but despite the urgency of the situation, Gloucester is happy to stay and "rot" where he is. Edgar scolds him for this repetition of his dark thoughts and says that a man must endure his fate **(Q1)**. Gloucester is still unaware that he is talking to his son.

QUOTES FROM ACT 5, SC. 1:

1 **REGAN**
I am doubtful that you have been conjunct
And bosomed with her, as far as we call hers.
EDMUND
No, by mine honour, madam. (12 — 14)

2 **REGAN**
                              Why is this reasoned?
GONERIL
Combine together 'gainst the enemy,
For these domestic and particular broils
Are not the question here. (28 — 31)

3 **EDMUND**
To both these sisters have I sworn my love,
Each jealous of the other as the stung
Are of the adder. (56 — 58)

4 **EDMUND**
                              As for the mercy
Which he intends to Lear and to Cordelia,
The battle done, and they within our power,
Shall never see his pardon; for my state
Stands on me to defend, not to debate. (66 — 70)

QUOTES FROM ACT 5, SC. 2:

1 **EDGAR**
What, in ill thoughts again? Men must endure
Their going hence even as their coming hither.
Ripeness is all. (9 — 11)

ACT 5, SC.3 (325 lines)

The British camp near Dover.

Assuming Albany's authority in victory, Edmund orders Lear and Cordelia to be taken away under guard. The defiant Cordelia tells Edmund that their defeat in battle does not prove them wrong **(Q1)**, and asks to see her sisters.

Lear, more stable than before, emphatically wishes to avoid any more contact with Goneril and Regan, and conjures up a romantic image of himself and Cordelia sharing a life in prison together **(Q2)**. Off they are marched, whilst Edmund stays behind to bribe a reluctant captain into murdering them both **(Q3)**.

As the captain leaves, Albany, Edmund, Goneril and Regan enter. Albany for the time being conceals his knowledge of the plot to kill him, and congratulates Edmund on his bravery. He asks him to send for Lear and Cordelia, but Edmund explains that he has put them under guard, as their fate was not an immediate priority in the aftermath of battle.

Albany reminds him that he has acted beyond his authority **(Q4)**, whereupon Regan and Goneril compete in leaping to his defence **(Q5)**. During the sisters' ensuing argument, Regan begins to feel unwell, but takes the opportunity publicly to declare Edmund her husband **(Q6)**. An altercation between him and Albany finally provokes the duke into arresting Edmund on a charge of capital treason. He forbids Edmund from marrying Regan on the premise, sarcastically, that he is already promised to Goneril – a marriage which, as her husband, he will not allow.

Then, as earlier requested by Edgar, he orders the trumpet to be sounded and throws down his gauntlet as a challenge to Edmund, to be taken up in the event that no other champion appears to prove his treasons **(Q7)**.

NOTES

_____

_____

_____

_____

_____

_____

QUOTES FROM ACT 5, SC. 3:

1   CORDELIA

We are not the first
Who with best meaning have incurred the worst. $(3-4)$

2   LEAR

No,no,no,no. Come, let's away to prison;
We two alone will sing like birds i'the cage.
When thou dost ask me blessing I'll kneel down
And ask of thee forgiveness. So we'll live
And pray, and sing, and tell old tales, and laugh... $(8-12)$

3   EDMUND

If thou dost
As this instructs thee, thou dost make thy way
To noble fortunes. Know thou this, that men
Are as the time is, to be tender-minded
Does not become a sword. $(29-33)$

4   ALBANY

Sir, by your patience,
I hold you but a subject of this war,
Not as a brother. $(60-62)$

5   REGAN

He led our powers,
Bore the commission of my place and person,
The which immediacy may well stand up
And call itself your brother.
GONERIL
Not so hot!
In his own grace he doth exalt himself
More than in your addition. $(64-69)$

6   REGAN

Witness the world, that I create thee here
My lord and master. $(78-79)$

7   ALBANY

If none appear to prove upon thy person
Thy heinous, manifest and many treasons,
There is my pledge. [Throws down his gauntlet.] $(29-33)$

Events gather pace as Regan sickens further, and an aside from Goneril tells the audience that she has poisoned her sister **(Q8)**. Edmund accepts the challenge, and Regan is carried to Albany's tent. At the third trumpet blast Edgar anonymously appears to uphold the challenge and, speaking once more as befits his rank, ceremoniously accuses his brother of being a traitor, disloyal to his family, and a conspirator against the duke **(Q9)**. Edmund rejects these accusations in like kind, they fight, and he falls, seriously wounded.

As the truth unravels, Goneril rushes off, pursued by one of Albany's officers. Edmund at last admits that the charges leveled at him were correct, and Edgar reveals his true identity. He tells of his escape, disguise, and his care of his father, having only revealed his identity to Gloucester half an hour previously, whereupon he died in a mixture of joy and grief **(Q10)**.

Perhaps as a delaying tactic to ensure that his orders regarding Lear and Cordelia are carried out, Edmund asks his brother to continue with his story. Edgar explains how Kent came upon him and his father's body, and how they exchanged revelations of what had occurred.

A messenger announces that Regan has died, poisoned by Goneril, who has in turn stabbed herself. Edmund jokes that the three of them will therefore soon be married **(Q11)**. Now Kent arrives, as the bodies of Goneril and Regan are produced **(Q12)**, to say that he has come to bid farewell to the king for ever. Suddenly Lear and Cordelia are remembered and, close to death, Edmund explains the situation **(Q13)**, causing immediate panic. Someone is despatched in haste to rescue them. Edmund explains that he and Goneril had arranged for the captain to hang Cordelia in semblance of suicide **(Q14)**.

NOTES

8 REGAN

　　　　　　Sick, O, sick!

GONERIL [*aside*]

If not, I'll ne'er trust medicine. (96 – 97)

9 EDGAR

False to thy gods, thy brother and thy father,
Conspirant 'gainst this high illustrious prince,
And from th'extremest upward of thy head
To the descent and dust below thy foot
A most toad-spotted traitor. (132 – 36)

10 EDGAR

　　　　　　But his flawed heart,
Alack, too weak the conflict to support,
'Twixt too extremes of passion, joy and grief,
Burst smilingly. (195 – 98)

11 EDMUND

I was contracted to them both; all three
Now marry in an instant. (227 – 28)

12 ALBANY

This judgement of the heavens that makes us tremble
Touches us not with pity... (230 – 31)

13 EDMUND

　　　　　　Quickly send –
Be brief in it – to the castle, for my writ
Is on the life of Lear and on Cordelia; (242 – 44)

14 EDMUND

He hath commission from thy wife and me
To hang Cordelia in the prison and
To lay the blame upon her own despair,
That she fordid herself. (250 – 53)

The rescue comes too late. Now Lear enters in despair with the body of Cordelia in his arms **(Q15)**. The scene is cataclysmic, reminiscent of the end of the world **(Q16)**. Lear desperately tries to find evidence of life in Cordelia, her breath upon a mirror, a feather stirring, but there is none. In a faint echo of "the dragon and his wrath" from the opening scene, he reveals that he killed the man who hanged her **(Q17)**. Turning to Kent, he begins vaguely to recognise him, but again loses his grip. Kent tries to explain matters to him, but he does not really understand **(Q18)**.

Edmund's death is announced, but that is of little significance after the tragedy which has just occurred **(Q19)**.

NOTES

15 LEAR
Howl, howl, howl, howl! O, you men of stones!
Had I your tongues and eyes, I'd use them so
That heaven's vault should crack: she's gone for ever. (255 — 57)

16 KENT
Is this the promised end?
EDGAR
Or image of that horror?
ALBANY
Fall, and cease. (261 — 62)

17 LEAR
I killed the slave that was a-hanging thee.
GENTLEMAN
'Tis true, my lords, he did.
LEAR
Did I not fellow?
I have seen the day, with my good biting falchion
I would have made him skip. (272 — 75)

18 KENT
                      All's cheerless, dark and deadly;
Your eldest daughters have fordone themselves
And desperately are dead.
LEAR
                      Ay, so I think.
ALBANY
He knows not what he says and vain is it
That we present us to him. (288 — 92)

19 MESSENGER [*to Albany*]
                      Edmund is dead, my Lord.
ALBANY
That's but a trifle here. (294)

Albany now tries, prematurely, to tie things up by passing on his regal authority to Lear, and restoring to Kent and Edgar their legitimate claims plus appropriate rewards. Idealistically, he attempts to apportion to each as he deserves **(Q20)**, but we know by now that in the real world such things do not happen. Of sole importance to Lear at this stage is the death of Cordelia **(Q21)**, and it is too much for him. In an echo of **3.iv.107**, he asks to be unbuttoned and then, imagining movement or a smile in her lips, dies. Did his heart "burst smilingly" as it did with Gloucester? We do not know for sure.

The trauma is finally over, and we unwind. "He faints" says Edgar. More realistically, Kent advises him to leave Lear in peace; his only comfort now is in death **(Q22)**. Albany, still trying to rescue order out of chaos, suggests that Edgar and Kent rule jointly in his stead, but even that satisfaction is withheld by Kent's admission that he does not have long to live **(Q23)**. The "general woe" remains unalleviated, and the play fizzles out quietly with Edgar's final comments **(Q24)**.

We are denied the artifice of a neat or significant conclusion. The characters limp on to who knows what new catastrophes, just like the rest of us.

NOTES

20 ALBANY

> *All friends shall taste*
> *The wages of their virtue and all foes*
> *The cup of their deservings.* (301−3)

21 LEAR

> *And my poor fool is hanged. No, no, no life!*
> *Why should a dog, a horse, a rat have life*
> *And thou no breath at all? O thou'lt come no more,*
> *Never, never, never, never, never.* (304−7)

22 KENT

> *Vex not his ghost; O, let him pass. He hates him*
> *That would upon the rack of this tough world*
> *Stretch him out longer.* (312−14)

23 KENT

> *I have a journey, sir, shortly to go;*
> *My master calls me, I must not say no.* (320−21)

24 EDGAR

> *The weight of this sad time we must obey,*
> *Speak what we feel, not what we ought to say.*
> *The oldest hath borne most;*
> *We that are young*
> *Shall never see so much, nor live so long.* (322−25)

NOTES

PURPLE PATCHES

1. ACT 1, SC. 1, 35-54

LEAR
Meantime we shall express our darker purpose.
Give me the map there. Know that we have divided
In three our kingdom, and 'tis our fast intent
To shake all cares and business from our age,
Conferring them on younger strengths while we
Unburdened crawl toward death. Our son of Cornwall,
And you, our no less loving son of Albany,
We have this hour a constant will to publish
Our daughters' several dowers, that future strife
May be prevented now.
The two great princes, France and Burgundy,
Great rivals in our youngest daughter's love,
Long in our court have made their amorous sojourn,
And here are to be answered. Tell me, my daughters -
Since now we will divest us both of rule,
Interest of territory, cares of state -
Which of you shall we say doth love us most
That we our largest bounty may extend
Where nature doth with merit challenge? - Goneril,
Our eldest born, speak first.

Context

This is Lear's first speech, and the one which causes all the trouble. It occurs shortly after Gloucester has been discussing his illegitimate son, Edmund, with Kent.

Afterwards, Lear's three daughters give him their various responses. Cordelia's naïve (or stubborn) honesty causes Lear to disinherit her and divide her share between Goneril and Regan. Kent bravely protests at this injustice, and is banished.

NOTES

2. ACT 1, SC. 2, 118–133

EDMUND

This is the excellent foppery of the world, that when we
are sick in fortune, often the surfeitof our own behaviour, we
make guilty of ourdisasters the sun, the moon, and the stars;
asif we were villains on necessity, fools by heavenly compulsion,
knaves, thieves, andtreachers by spherical predominance;
drunkards,liars and adulterers by an enforced obedience of
planetary influence; and all that we are evil in, by a divine
thrusting on. An admirable evasion of whoremaster man, to lay
his goatishdisposition on the charge of a star! My father
compounded with my mother under the dragon's tail, and my
nativity was under Ursa major, so that it follows I am rough and
lecherous. Fut! I should have been that I am had the maidenliest
star in the firmament twinkled on my bastardising.

Context

Having been introduced briefly to Edmund in the previous scene, we now find out what makes him tick. He will use whatever means he has at his disposal to disinherit his legitimate brother Edgar, and gain the benefit himself. Unlike his father, he has no time for astrology, nor any other such beliefs not rooted in the real world.

Afterwards, we witness the discord created between Lear and Goneril by his sojourn in her palace, and the unruly behavior, she claims, of his retainers.

NOTES

3. ACT 1, SC. 4, 120-148

FOOL

Nuncle, give me an egg, and I'll give thee two crowns.

LEAR

What two crowns shall they be?

FOOL

Why, after I have cut the egg i'th'middle and eat up the meat, the two crowns of the egg. When thou clovest thy crown i'th'middle, and gavest away both parts, thou bor'st thine ass on thy back o'er the dirt. Thou hadst little wit in thy bald crown when thou gav'st thy golden one away. If I speak like myself in this, let him be whipped that first finds it so.

(sings)

> Fools had ne'er less grace in a year,
> For wise men are grown foppish.
> They know not how their wits to wear,
>   Their manners are so apish.

LEAR

When were you wont to be so full of songs, sirrah?

FOOL

I have used it, nuncle, e'er since thou mad'st thy daughters thy mothers. For when thou gav'st them the rod, and put'st down thine own breeches,

(sings)

> Then they for sudden joy did weep
> And I for sorrow sung,
> That such a king should play bo-peep
> And go the fools among.

Prithee, nuncle, keep a schoolmaster that can teach thy fool to lie. I would fain learn to lie.

LEAR

An you lie, sirrah, we'll have you whipped.

FOOL

I marvel what kin thou and thy daughters are. They'll have me whipped for speaking true, thou'lt have me whipped for lying, and sometimes I am whipped for holding my peace. I had rather be any kind o'thing than a fool. And yet I would not be thee, nuncle. Thou hast pared thy wit o'both sides and left nothing i'th'middle. Here comes one o'the parings.

In Goneril's palace, Kent, ignoring his banishment, has disguised himself and offered his services to Lear out of a loyal sense of protection. He has just ridiculed and tripped up Goneril's insolent servant, Oswald, much to Lear's satisfaction. They are joined by the fool, who clearly believes that Lear has acted unwisely in unburdening himself of his possessions to his two elder daughters.

There follows a confrontation between Lear and Goneril, who has been spoiling for a fight, and who tells Lear to reduce the number of his retainers from a hundred to fifty. This is not well received.

NOTES

4. ACT 2, SC. 2, 453–475

LEAR

O, reason not the need! Our basest beggars
Are in the poorest thing superfluous.
Allow not nature more than nature needs,
Man's life's as cheap as beast's. Thou art a lady.
If only to go warm were gorgeous,
Why, nature needs not what thou gorgeous wear'st,
Which scarcely keeps thee warm. But, for true need—
You heavens, give me that patience, patience I need.
You see me here, you gods, a poor old man,
As full of grief as age, wretched in both.
If it be you that stir these daughters' hearts
Against their father, fool me not so much
To bear it tamely. Touch me with noble anger.
And let not women's weapons, water drops,
Stain my man's cheeks! No, you unnatural hags,
I will have such revenges on you both
That all the world shall—I will do such things—
What they are yet I know not, but they shall be
The terrors of the earth. You think I'll weep?
No, I'll not weep.

Storm and tempest

I have full cause of weeping, but this heart
Shall break into a hundred thousand flaws,
Or e'er I'll weep. O fool, I shall go mad.

Context

At Gloucester's castle, Kent has been put in the stocks by Cornwall, and Goneril and Regan, acting together, have been exerting their power over Lear by insisting on a reduction in his retinue. Goneril has just asked him why he even needs one retainer.

A storm is brewing and, his outburst complete, they shut their aged father out of Gloucester's castle and leave him at the mercy of the elements.

NOTES

---

5. ACT 3, SC. 2, 1-64

LEAR

Blow, winds, and crack your cheeks! Rage, blow!
You cataracts and hurricanoes, spout
Till you have drenched our steeples, drowned the cocks!
You sulfurous and thought-executing fires,
Vaunt-couriers of oak-cleaving thunderbolts,
Singe my white head! And thou, all-shaking thunder,
Smite flat the thick rotundity o'th'world,
Crack nature's moulds, all germens spill at once
That make ingrateful man!

FOOL

O nuncle, court holy water in a dry house is better than this
rainwater out o'door. Good nuncle, in, and ask thy daughters
blessing. Here's a night pities neither wise man nor fools.

LEAR

Rumble thy bellyful! Spit, fire! Spout, rain!
Nor rain, wind, thunder, fire are my daughters.
I tax not you, you elements, with unkindness.
I never gave you kingdom, called you children.
You owe me no subscription. Why then, let fall
Your horrible pleasure. Here I stand, your slave,
A poor, infirm, weak, and despised old man.
But yet I call you servile ministers,
That will with two pernicious daughters join
Your high engendered battles 'gainst a head
So old and white as this. Oh, ho! 'Tis foul.

NOTES

---

6. ACT 3, SC. 2, 78–95

FOOL

This is a brave night to cool a courtesan. I'll speak a
prophecy ere I go:
When priests are more in word than matter,
When brewers mar their malt with water,
When nobles are their tailors' tutors,
No heretics burned but wenches' suitors,
Then shall the realm of Albion
Come to great confusion.
When every case in law is right,
No squire in debt nor no poor knight;
When slanders do not live in tongues,
Nor cutpurses come not to throngs;
When usurers tell their gold i'th'field,
And bawds and whores do churches build,
Then comes the time, who lives to see't,
That going shall be used with feet.
This prophecy Merlin shall make, for I live before his time.

NOTES

---

7. ACT 3, SC. 4, 11-36

LEAR

                   ...When the mind's free,
The body's delicate. This tempest in my mind
Doth from my senses take all feeling else
Save what beats there: filial ingratitude.
Is it not as this mouth should tear this hand
For lifting food to't? But I will punish home.
No, I will weep no more. In such a night
To shut me out! Pour on, I will endure.
In such a night as this! O Regan, Goneril,
Your old kind father, whose frank heart gave all -
Oh, that way madness lies. Let me shun that.
No more of that.

KENT

Good my lord, enter here.

LEAR

Prithee, go in thyself. Seek thine own ease.
This tempest will not give me leave to ponder
On things would hurt me more. But I'll go in.
(to FOOL) In, boy. Go first. You houseless poverty—
Nay, get thee in. I'll pray, and then I'll sleep.
                         [exit Fool]
Poor naked wretches, whereso'er you are,
That bide the pelting of this pitiless storm,
How shall your houseless heads and unfed sides,
Your looped and windowed raggedness, defend you
From seasons such as these? Oh, I have ta'en
Too little care of this! Take physic, pomp.
Expose thyself to feel what wretches feel,
That thou mayst shake the superflux to them
And show the heavens more just.

Immediately following Gloucester's revelation to Edmund, we are returned to the storm on the heath and Lear, who, as this speech demonstrates, is beginning to show consideration for others.

They then encounter Poor Tom (the disguised Edgar) in the hovel, and the deterioration of Lear's mind continues.

NOTES

---

8. ACT 3, SC. 4, 91–7

LEAR

Why, thou wert better in thy grave than to answer with thy uncovered body this extremity of the skies. Is man no more than this? Consider him well. Thou ow'st the worm no silk, the beast no hide, the sheep no wool, the cat no perfume. Ha! Here's three on's are sophisticated. Thou art the thing itself. Unaccommodated man is no more but such a poor, bare, forked animal as thou art. Off, off, you lendings! Come. Unbutton here. *(tears at his clothes)*

Context

This important scene continues, and Lear addresses the naked Poor Tom, just before Gloucester finds them and offers help, and warns Kent of the plot against the king's life.

NOTES

---

9. ACT 4, SC. 6, 103-129

GLOUCESTER
The trick of that voice I do well remember:
Is 't not the king?

KING LEAR
Ay, every inch a king:
When I do stare, see how the subject quakes.
I pardon that man's life. What was thy cause? Adultery?
Thou shalt not die: die for adultery? No:
The wren goes to't, and the small gilded fly
Does lecher in my sight.
Let copulation thrive: for Gloucester's bastard son
Was kinder to his father than my daughters
Got 'tween the lawful sheets.
To't, luxury, pell-mell! for I lack soldiers.
Behold yond simp'ring dame,
Whose face between her forks presages snow;
That minces virtue, and does shake the head
To hear of pleasure's name;
The fitchew, nor the soiled horse, goes to 't
With a more riotous appetite.
Down from the waist they are Centaurs,
Though women all above:
But to the girdle do the gods inherit,
Beneath is all the fiend's.
There's hell, there's darkness, there is the sulphurous pit,
burning, scalding, stench, consumption. Fie,fie, fie! Pah, pah!
Give me an ounce of civet, good apothecary, to sweeten my
imagination: there's money for thee.

GLOUCESTER
O, let me kiss that hand!

KING LEAR
Let me wipe it first; it smells of mortality.

Edgar has frustrated his father's attempt at suicide, and a mad Lear, garlanded with a crown of flowers, has entered upon the scene. Gloucester, now blind, thinks he recognizes the king's voice.

NOTES

---

10. ACT 4, SC. 6, 152–165

LEAR
Thou rascal beadle, hold thy bloody hand.
Why dost thou lash that whore? Strip thine own back.
Thou hotly lusts to use her in that kind
For which thou whip'st her. The usurer hangs the cozener.
Through tattered clothes great vices do appear:
Robes and furred gowns hide all. Plate sin with gold,
And the strong lance of justice hurtless breaks;
Arm it in rags, a pigmy's straw does pierce it.
None does offend, none, I say, none. I'll able 'em.
Take that of me, my friend, who have the power
To seal th'accuser's lips. Get thee glass eyes,
And like a scurvy politician, seem
To see the things thou dost not. Now, now, now, now,
Pull off my boots. Harder, harder! So.

11. ACT 4, SC. 7, 57–67

LEAR
I am a very foolish fond old man,
Fourscore and upward, not an hour more nor less.
And to deal plainly
I fear I am not in my perfect mind.
Methinks I should know you, and know this man.
Yet I am doubtful, for I am mainly ignorant
What place this is, and all the skill I have
Remembers not these garments. Nor I know not
Where I did lodge last night. Do not laugh at me,
For as I am a man, I think this lady
To be my child Cordelia.

CORDELIA
And so I am, I am.

LEAR
Be your tears wet? Yes, faith. I pray, weep not.
If you have poison for me, I will drink it.
I know you do not love me, for your sisters
Have, as I do remember, done me wrong.
You have some cause; they have not.

CORDELIA
No cause, no cause.

This occurs later in the same scene, after which Lear runs off, chased by his attendants. Oswald – who has been asked by Regan to kill Gloucester on sight - chances upon Gloucester and Edgar. In the ensuing sword-fight, Oswald is killed, and Edgar discovers letters on him which reveal Goneril's desire to kill Albany and supplant him with Edmund as her husband.

Context

The battle between the French and English armies draws near, and Cordelia has thanked Kent for his loyal and honourable conduct towards Lear. They await his awakening. When he wakes up, Lear's confused state of mind, and admission of his wrongs, help the touching reconciliation between him and Cordelia.

12. ACT 5, SC. 3, 279–291

LEAR
And my poor fool is hanged. No, no, no life?
Why should a dog, a horse, a rat have life,
And thou no breath at all? Thou'lt come no more,
Never, never, never, never, never.
Pray you, undo this button. Thank you, sir.
Do you see this? Look on her. Look, her lips.
Look there, look there.   *(He dies)*

EDGAR
                              He faints. My lord, my lord.

KENT
Break, heart, I prithee break.

EDGAR
                              Look up, my lord.

KENT
Vex not his ghost. O, let him pass. He hates him
That would upon the rack of this tough world
Stretch him out longer.

EDGAR
                              He is gone indeed.

KENT
The wonder is he hath endured so long.
He but usurped his life.

N➔TES

NOTES

INDEX

INDEX

ACT 2

ACT 3

INDEX

NOTES

SHOTS SHAKESPEARE
Straight to the point